THE PENGUIN CLASSICS

FOUNDER EDITOR (1944–64): E. V. RIEU

· EDITORS:
Robert Baldick (1964-72)
Betty Radice
C. A. Jones

WANG WEI (?699–?761) flourished in the mid T'ang period, generally regarded as the apogee of Chinese civilization. He was precociously talented, and esteemed in his lifetime for his poetry, painting, and music, though it is only as a poet that he can now be known. He had a successful career in the civil service and enjoyed metropolitan and court life, but his most characteristic poetry reflects his deep feeling for the natural world and for rural seclusion. He was a practising Buddhist and his tone of voice, compared with that of his great contemporaries, Li Po and Tu Fu, is quiet.

G. W. ROBINSON had a classical education up to the age of nineteen. He served in the army for six years during the Second World War, in the course of which he learned some Japanese. He subsequently studied classical Chinese, and then specialized in the ancient history of Japan. After a year in Japan he was for a short period a lecturer in Far Eastern History at the School of Oriental and African studies in London. He has lived in the Languedoc since 1957.

POEMS OF WANG WEI

TRANSLATED WITH AN INTRODUCTION
BY G. W. ROBINSON

PENGUIN BOOKS

Penguin Books Ltd, Harmondsworth, Middlesex, England
Penguin Books Inc., 7110 Ambassador Road, Baltimore, Maryland 21207, U.S.A.
Penguin Books Australia Ltd, Ringwood, Victoria, Australia

This translation first published 1973

Copyright © G. W. Robinson, 1973

Made and printed in Great Britain by
Hazell Watson & Viney Ltd,
Aylesbury, Bucks
Set in Monotype Fournier

To Barbara

CONTENTS

Preface 9

Select Bibliography 11

Introduction 13

POEMS OF WANG WEI 27

Appendix I
A letter to P'ei Ti from the hills 141

Appendix II
*The story of the Peach Blossom Spring
by T'ao Ch'ien (T'ao Yüan-ming)* 143

PREFACE

MANY visiting friends, over recent years, have been pestered by me to read and, if possible, to enjoy various drafts of these translations; and those who know Chinese have often been put to work. I hope that they will recognize themselves and accept my gratitude, unnamed, lest they should incur, along with the credit that I accord them, any discredit, which is mine alone. But I must name, with equal thanks, my friend and neighbour Madame Gabriel Guet, for managing to fit the typing of this book into her busy summer life.

Thanks are also due to the following for permission to quote from the works named: David Hawkes and the Oxford University Press, *Ch'u Tzu: Songs of the South*; Messrs George Allen & Unwin Limited, *The Analects of Confucius* and *The Book of Songs*, by Arthur Waley.

I am also most grateful to Mr Akio Sawa of Osaka, who, though quite unknown to me, heard of my need and sent me his copy of Kobayashi Taichirō's valuable and unobtainable book on Wang Wei's life and art, in time for me to make use of it.

Finally I must thank the proprietors of the periodical, *Art and Literature*, for permission to reprint here the following poems which appeared in the same, or nearly the same, form in their pages: poems on pages 27–32, 57, 59, 60, 63, 65, 69, 71, 79, 86, 87, 100, 101, 104, 110, 123, 130; and *The Times Literary Supplement* for similar permission in respect of the poems on pages 42, 43, 46, 73, 75, 77.

Vic-le-Fesq (Gavd)
September 1972   G. W. ROBINSON

SELECT BIBLIOGRAPHY

THE following books are referred to in the introduction and notes:

Jerome Ch'en and Michael Bullock: *Poems of Solitude* (Abelard-Schuman, 1960).

A. R. Davis: (introduction to) *The Penguin Book of Chinese Verse* (Penguin Books, 1962).

Paul Demiéville: (introduction to) *Anthologie de la poésie classique chinoise* (Gallimard, 1962).

A. C. Graham: *Poems of the Late T'ang* (Penguin Classics, 1965).

David Hawkes: *Ch'u Tzu: Songs of the South* (Oxford University Press, 1959).

James J. Y. Liu: *The Art of Chinese Poetry* (Routledge & Kegan Paul, 1962).

James J. Y. Liu: *The Poetry of Li Shang-yin* (Columbia University Press, 1969).

Arthur Waley: *The Analects of Confucius* (George Allen & Unwin, 1938).

Arthur Waley: *The Book of Songs* (George Allen & Unwin, 1937).

Burton Watson: *Chinese Lyricism: Shih Poems from the Second to the Twelfth Century* (Columbia University Press, 1971).

*

Ch'en I-hsin: *Wang Wei Shih-hsüan* (Jenmin Wenhsüeh Ch'upan She, 1959).

Tsuru Haruo: *Ō I* (no. 6 of the *Chūgoku Shijin Senshū*, Iwanami Shoten, 1958).

Kobayashi Taichirō: *Ō I no Shōgai to Geijutsu* (Zenkoku Shobō, 1944).

INTRODUCTION

I

WANG WEI (699–761)* is one of the great poets. His distinction would no doubt be more widely recognized, outside China and Japan, had he not flourished during a period universally regarded as one in which Chinese poetry reached a zenith, dominated by the reputations of Li Po (701–62) and Tu Fu (712–70). Their passions were overt: Li Po's might be called a kind of romanticism, Tu Fu's, in modern parlance, 'involvement'. Their poetry may speak more directly to western people today than that of the inwardly passionate, contemplative Wang Wei. But this situation is perhaps even now changing.

Though material exists for a fairly full account of Wang Wei's life,† only the salient features need, or, indeed, can, be given here.

He was born in Shansi, of a respectable family, his father a local official, his mother member of a family (the Ts'ui) of distinguished *littérateurs*. At the age of about sixteen, with his brother, Chin, a year younger, he arrived in the capital. The brothers' precocious and exceptional talents gained them early *entrée* to the highest, princely society. (Poems on pp. 34–6, 73,

---

*These dates will surprise. But those usually given, 699–759 or 701–61, are, in both cases, inconsistent with available evidence. 699–761 perhaps constitutes the best compromise; but this is a matter of small importance.

†The first part of Kobayashi's book is such an account, though probably susceptible of expansion. Ch'en I-hsin's postface to his selection may be valuable to the reader accustomed to dealing with Marxist procrusteanism. There is no such account that I know of in English.

102, 105 and, probably, 46 belong to this youthful period.) After graduation to the degree of *chin-shih* at the age of twenty-three, Wang Wei was fortunate enough to receive immediately the court appointment of Assistant Secretary for Music. But for some reason or other – perhaps for having a dancer take a role exclusively reserved for the emperor – he was almost at once sent off to a minor provincial post in Shantung (poem p. 39). He put up with this only for a few years before resigning from the service and returning to the metropolitan area. About this time, partly, perhaps, because he could not afford the life of the capital while out of office, and also, surely, because he was already attracted to the pure and tranquil life of the country, he bought his famous estate on the Wang River, at the eastern end of the mountains variously known as the Chungnan range or the Southern Mountains, about thirty miles south of Ch'angan, the capital. This acquisition was momentous for his poetry, of which it became a constant subject. (See the first twenty poems in this selection, and numerous others.) He lived there on and off, whenever he was unemployed or on holiday, for the rest of his life.

But soon after this occurred the first great tragedy in his life. He was only a little more than thirty when his wife died, and, though he had no children, he never remarried. The poem on p. 117 was probably written soon after this.

After a period of solitude following on this loss, he again entered the public service in 734, thanks to the personal intervention of his friend Chang Chiu-ling, then prime minister, an excellent poet, and one of the last honest statesmen of this period. In spite of the fall of Chang Chiu-ling some three years later, due to the intrigues of Li Lin-fu, who succeeded him, Wang Wei somehow managed to continue in office, without rupture of his relations with his former sponsor (poem p. 92). Among other activities, he went on a mission to the north-west frontier in 737, which lasted two or three years and which, for us, means a number of poems about this savage region, as seen by this most visual of poets (e.g. pp. 95, 96, 108, etc.). Soon after his return from this mission, he seems to have gone off again, to South China, in 740, when Meng Hao-jan, a very fine poet senior to him, but most congenial, had just died (poem p. 45).

His undistinguished official life continued, with periods of holiday at his Lant'ien estate on the Wang River. Then, about 749 or 750, came the second great tragedy of his life, the death of his mother, who had lived on his estate until then, whom he loved deeply, through whom he had probably inherited his great gifts, and with whom he shared deep Buddhist beliefs. He again resigned from the service and performed the proper three years of mourning with the saddest and most ascetic sincerity and thoroughness. He movingly petitioned the emperor for permission, which he received, to convert his mother's house on his estate into a temple.

Not long after he resumed office, in about 752 or 753, the rebellion of An Lu-shan, in 755, broke the long T'ang peace of nearly one and a half centuries. For one reason or another, probably illness, Wang Wei was unable to follow the court in its flight to Szechwan, and was captured by the rebels. He is said to have tried to commit suicide and to have pretended to be a deaf mute. It is wonderful that he was not put to death. He eventually succumbed to pressure, and accepted office in the rebel government. When the imperial forces recaptured the capital in 757, he was lucky to escape execution. But his brother, Chin, whose record during this time had been excellent, interceded for him, and it is also said that the poems on pp. 115 and 116 were placed to his credit. He continued, therefore, in office, reaching his highest position in the Council of State, something like that of a deputy-minister, about two years before he died.

The position was, in full, that of *Shangshu Yuch'eng*, and

15

he is frequently referred to, therefore, as Wang Yuch'eng. In August 761 he knew that death was approaching him, old and ill as he was, and he is said to have died while writing farewells to his brother, Chin, and his friends.

So far there may seem to be nothing to distinguish him from thousands of reasonably successful Chinese civil servants. There is even the smell of the *bien pensant* about one who managed to weather palace revolutions and a bloody rebellion unscathed. The fact is that he was not ambitious for worldly success; he probably only held office for social and financial reasons. He was not interested, not 'involved'. Something of what did interest him is plainly stated in his letter to P'ei Ti (appendix I), and this was the material that his genius used, or, it might almost be said, used his genius.

2

It is of prime importance that Wang Wei was a practising and believing Buddhist, as were his mother and brothers (nothing is known about his father in this respect). He chose as his 'style' (*tzu*) the characters pronounced *mo-chieh*, which, preceded by his given name, Wei, produce the Chinese for the name of the Buddhist saint, Vimalakīrti. His most characteristic and personal poetry is permeated by a genuine Buddhist quietism, quite often explicitly expressed. The idea of mankind as just one constituent of the whole natural order, rather than as in some sort of special opposition to it, is a natural tendency in Chinese thought and is particularly essential to Wang Wei's kind of Buddhism. And so his delicately observed, though at the same time generalized, descriptions of landscape, for which he is most famous, are able to move us, whether ostensibly peopled or not, because of the intensity of the poet's own presence. His observation of nature was not objective, nor that of an aesthete, because he was himself a part of nature, and it is this integrality that he celebrates. And if the ideal of his kind of Buddhism is a kind of total passivity, then the very act of writing poems must have seemed to him, in some moods, to have constituted a violation of the ideal, a kind of failure. This must surely be the interpretation of the poem I have chosen to end this selection, especially the lines,

> In a past life I was mistakenly a poet
> In a former existence I must have been a painter
> Unable to throw off my remnant habits.

His *karma* is too strong for him.

The ability not only to support solitude but positively to enjoy and use it is an almost invariable attribute of genius. Wang Wei, though most powerfully attached to his family and friends, relished solitude also, the condition indeed in which, alone, his religious aspirations could be fully realized, and in which his sense of belonging to the whole creation was naturally at its deepest. This is the significance of such a poem as 'Bamboo Grove House' (p. 31) where he says that no one knows where he is,

> 'But the bright moon comes and shines on me there

Similarly, he says, when in a strange part of the country, where the dialect was unintelligible,

> ... the orioles sounded as in my own country
> And luckily I know about landscape
> And that abated my feeling of isolation.

> (p. 72)

In such a case the solitude was not of his seeking, but it stimulated him to write poetry; and the enforced loneliness brought on him by the loss first of his wife and later of his mother inspired much poignant writing.

The symbolic or metaphorical values in many of these personal poems are generally plain enough to need no par-

17

ticular comment here. But there is one expression which recurs no less than ten times in this small selection of poems: 'white clouds'. In nearly every case it is clear that these simple words have an important non-literal significance. I have grouped nine of these poems together (pp. 60–9), so that the reader may the more conveniently form his own idea. (The tenth poem concerned is 'Lake I', on page 29.) My own feeling is that the white clouds or, sometimes, *beyond* the white clouds, represent some incorporeal, ideally pure country of the spirit; however, it is unlikely that this, or anything else, was ever more than vaguely formulated in the poet's mind.

The somewhat crass and distasteful term, 'nature poet' (and the Chinese or Japanese equivalent), is sometimes applied to Wang Wei. But was he not, in the type of work so far discussed, rather a religious or mystical poet?

Though not ambitious for worldly success or political power, he had his worldly side. Much of his life was spent at court, where there were not only his official duties to be performed, but also numerous and elaborate social functions, banquets, progresses and so forth, to be attended. So his extant work includes quite a large number of court poems, generally written at imperial or princely command. These are generally very skilful but they usually lack personal feeling; they tend, moreover, to be crammed with more or less recondite allusions, which today require extensive annotation, even for Chinese or Japanese readers, and would, for this reason alone, be unsuitable in a selection like this one. I have included two such poems by way of illustration: a command poem (p. 57), and a rather elaborate farewell to Ch'ao Heng (p. 134), who, though a friend, does not seem to have been an intimate one. (I chose the latter partly for the adventitious interest of its being addressed to a Japanese, who had become an official of the T'ang bureaucracy.)

Many poems reflect the unresolved conflict in Wang Wei's

mind between the worldly and the mystical sides of his nature, and also – this is, of course, felt by sincere adherents of many religions – the incompatibility of strong human affections with the religious ideal. Much in the world impelled him towards mysticism; but the friends and the wine cups held him in the world. Few men so richly endowed with such diverse talents could easily forego the position in the highest society that these talents had earned him at an early stage. This is what Kobayashi means by his deliberately startling opening to his critical discussion of Wang Wei: that he was a great ('high') man but also an ordinary one. And he goes on to attribute to Wang Wei a sense of guilt or self-disgust at being part of the world that disgusted him. I find this rather too strong. I believe that he simply recognized, and on the whole resigned himself to, his inner conflict as such. So at times we find him envying a friend retiring to the country, at times hankering for high society in the tones of one buried in the remotest province, rather than a mere day's journey from Ch'angan, often receiving visits. There may occasionally be an element of fashionable posing here, since these attitudes were often struck by Chinese poets, but one senses on the whole the sincerity of a genuine conflict.

Nor do I agree in finding abject self-disgust in his petition to the emperor for the return of his loved brother, Chin, to a post in the capital. He argues, rhetorically but with some truth, his own inferiority to his brother in the qualities traditionally held essential for a gentleman and official. His motive was simply a longing to see his brother before his own imminent death. (Though his request was granted, it seems probable that Chin did not arrive in time.)

3

Wang Wei was at least as celebrated in his lifetime as a painter, as he was as a poet. We can only accept the verdict of his contemporaries and of later critics, who extolled him even more highly, since, with the conceivable exception of a single portrait, no work of his survives. His poetry indeed suggests an intense interest in the incidence of light, in differences of shade and in the 'lay-out' of vast landscapes. And descriptions of his paintings do imply that he participated in a movement, already begun in the seventh century, towards a liberation of the art of landscape painting, though he was also well known as a painter of portraits, both of contemporaries and of sages of antiquity (including, of course, Vimalakīrti). Later generations revered him as the father of the so-called Southern School, as opposed to General Li Ssŭ-hsün (651–716), who was claimed by the Northern School, but there is no indication that these two offered a marked contrast in the eyes of Wang Wei's contemporaries – and, in general, in all the arts, stylistic contrasts tend to become blurred for posterity. No doubt Kobayashi is right in suggesting that Wang Wei was claimed as the spiritual father of the Southern School, without specific stylistic reference. He became the archetype of that revered figure, the Scholar-Painter.

However, there does seem some reason for believing that he originated the idea of painting a landscape on a long horizontal scroll, in which case he has the credit for an important extension of the scope of Chinese landscape painting. The twenty scenes evoked in the quatrains of the Wang River Sequence, with which this selection opens, were depicted by him on such a scroll, generally known as the Wang River Scroll. Unfortunately none of the surviving paraphrases of this scroll is earlier than 1617, the date of a late Ming engraved version; and this version must be at many removes from the original in view of the discrepancies in the order of the scenes, as between the poems and the engraving. The painted scroll in the British Museum, though ostensibly dated 1309 and ascribed to the famous Yüan dynasty artist, Chao Meng-fu, should in truth be attributed to the mid seventeenth century. Thus these paraphrases may tell us something of the topography of Wang Wei's surroundings by the Wang River, but they can give us no idea of his style as a painter.

4

The verse form used by Wang Wei and his contemporaries, and by their predecessors and successors, was the *shih*. These poems generally consist of a series of five-syllable lines or of seven-syllable lines, of which the even-numbered lines rhyme. Poems of four-syllable lines and six-syllable lines exist but are much less common. By the time Wang Wei was writing there were two styles of *shih*: the *ku-shih* or *ku-t'i* or 'old-style verse'; and the *chin-t'i – shih* or 'modern-style verse', also known as *lü-shih* or 'regulated verse'. The modern style had been developed during the seventh century, and, as its alternative name implies, was subject to more rigorous rules than the old style. The basic *lü-shih* had eight lines, all of the same length, a matter in which some liberty was allowed in the old style. A single rhyme had to be used throughout the poem, whereas it could be changed at will in the old style. The various tones of the spoken language being classifiable as 'level' or 'oblique', certain tone patterns were imposed. The most important requirement was such that the second line of a couplet had generally to be a tonal reciprocal of the first, as illustrated in the example below. But since it is impossible to reproduce the various tonal intricacies in translation, this is not the place to examine them more thoroughly.*

One aspect of the new style which it is, however, sometimes possible to reproduce without undue strain, is the requirement that the third and fourth couplets should present perfect grammatical parallelism and semantic antithesis or parallelism. An example will best explain this: the central couplets of the poem on p. 75 are:

> Bright moon shining between pines
> Clear stream flowing over stones
> Bamboos clatter – the washerwoman goes home
> Lotuses shift – the fisherman's boat floats down.

In the original this was:

(— = level tone   / = oblique tone)

ming	yüeh	sung	chien	chao
/	/	—	—	—
bright	moon	pines	between	shine
ch'ing	chüan	shih	shang	liu
—	—	/	/	—
clear	stream	stones	over	flow
chu	hsüan	kuei	huan	nü
/	—	—	/	/
bamboo(s)	clatter	home	washer	woman (or women)
lien	tung	hsia	yü	chou
/	/	/	—	—
lotus(es)	shift	down	fisher-	boat(s)

(Note that both 'home' and 'down' are verbs here.) The first of these couplets is particularly admired by connoisseurs. The

*For full discussion, see the books of Davis, Demiéville, Liu and Watson. Liu, in *The Art of Chinese Poetry*, often uses Wang Wei's work for illustrative purposes, while Watson, pp. 169–76, discusses this poet and provides a number of translations. One of Wang Wei's poems appears in Davis's anthology, seven in Demiéville's.

poet has allowed himself a licence in the tone of the first syllable of the second couplet, which should strictly have been a level tone. Such licence may be taken here, but never with the rhyming syllable.

The new style embraced two other forms, the *p'ai-lü* and the *chüeh-chü*. In the former, any number of antithetical couplets could be interposed between the opening and closing couplets, while the latter were quatrains in which obedience to the rules of tonal reciprocality was required.

In all *shih*, old and new, there is a strong caesura, of sense as well as sound, after the second syllable of a five-syllable line, and after the fourth of a seven-syllable line. The latter is represented here by breaking the lines into two parts as in, for example, the poem on pp. 34–6. All lines not so printed are of five syllables, unless otherwise noted. It should also be re-marked that the sense always stops, or, at least, pauses, at the end of each line, and most translators have generally found it most satisfactory to follow the original lineation, as I have nearly always done here.

Old-style poems have been noted as such here in the hope that, sometimes at least, their comparative looseness of texture may be apparent; however, the parallelism or antithesis required in the new style is by no means always absent from the old, since these are constant features of Chinese writing, both verse and prose, from the earliest times.

It is worth remarking that, while Wang Wei's extant work is about equally divided between the two styles, only a little more than a quarter of this selection is old style. A rather similar disproportion is found in the Chinese and Japanese selections listed. Assuming that each anthologist aimed to offer what he considered the best of Wang Wei, as I have done, we may suppose that this poet was generally stimulated to fashion his finest work by the exigencies of the new style, rather than by the comparative freedom of the old.

5

Rather more than four hundred poems by Wang Wei survive. They were collected after his death, on imperial order, by Wang Chin, then prime minister. Wang Chin said that his brother had composed 'hundreds and thousands' of poems but that the troubles of the time – the rebellions of An Lu-shan and Shih Ssŭ-ming – had caused them to be dispersed, and less than one in ten survived. Even allowing for fraternal exaggeration, our loss is great.

This selection, then, constitutes rather more than a quarter of the surviving work, and is based purely on my personal preference. The problems facing a translator of classical Chinese poetry are formidable, and it is arguable that no poet poses them more acutely than does Wang Wei. But rather than discuss them here, I would refer the reader to Professor Liu's two books, the former of which is indispensable for anyone interested in Chinese poetry, and to the masterly discussion by Professor Graham in his introduction to *Poems of the Late T'ang*. But I should make it clear that I am rash enough to disagree with Professor Liu, bilingual though he be, as to the necessity of always using conventional English grammar and syntax. I have tried, intermittently, to reproduce the peculiar density and deliberate imprecision of the original language by the omission of many grammatical nuts and bolts, as well as by minimal punctuation. I hope that I have not thereby produced language which sounds 'like telegrams or newspaper headlines'.*

The annotation is far from exhaustive, but I hope that it is generally adequate for the understanding of each poem. Some notes, though not essential, are included for their intrinsic interest.

*Liu, *The Poetry of Li Shang-yin*, p. 40.

The order of the poems is arbitrary: too few can be dated for a chronological scheme to be followed, while the traditional arrangement according to style and length of line leads to monotony.

After each poem or sequence of poems is given the number of the *chüan* (i.e. 'book' or 'section') in which it appears in *Wang Yuch'eng Chi Chienchu*, published by Chao Tien-ch'eng in 1736, and available in numerous subsequent editions.

THE WANG RIVER SEQUENCE

My country retreat is in the hill valley of the Wang River. There are pleasant walks among such places as Meng Wall Hollow, Huatzu Hill, Apricot Wood House, Bamboo Hill, Deer Park, Magnolia Park, Dogwood Bank, Sophora Walk, Lake Pavilion, South Hill, Lake I, Willow Waves, the Rapids by the Luans', Gold Dust Spring, White Stone Shallows, North Hill, Bamboo Grove House, Magnolia Slope, Lacquer Garden and Pepper Garden. P'ei Ti and I occupied our leisure in writing quatrains about these places.

Meng Wall Hollow

New home near this Meng Wall
Old trees – some dying willows still –
And who will live here in the future
To grieve vainly for him that was here before?

Huatzu Hill

Flying birds away into endless spaces
Ranged hills all autumn colours again.
I go up Huatzu Hill and come down –
Will my sadness never come to its end?

Apricot Wood House

Straight-grained apricot cut to make the beams
Fragrant reeds woven to make the roof
Perhaps clouds do form in these rafters
And go and make rain among men.

Bamboo Hill

Tall bamboos reflected in the meandering water
So the rippling river drifts blue and green
We are on the Shang Mountain track unobserved —
Something no woodman would understand.

Deer Park

Hills empty, no one to be seen
We only hear voices echoed —
With light coming back into the deep wood
The top of the green moss is lit again.

Magnolia Park

Autumn hills taking the last of the light
Birds flying, mate following mate
Brilliant greens here and there distinct
Evening mists have no resting place.

Dogwood Bank

The fruit is forming red and yet green
And it is as if flowers were opening again
If I detain a visitor in these hills
I may offer him this dogwood cup.

Sophora Walk

It is a by-path sheltered by sophoras
Much is green moss in the secret shade
The gateman respectfully sweeps it in case
A monk from the hill comes to call.

Lake Pavilion

Light boat to meet the honoured guest
Far far advancing over the lake –
We gain the balcony and sit with our wine
And lotuses are opening all about.

South Hill

My light boat can get to South Hill
North hill is hard, the water wide
On the other shore we can make out houses
Far far, people we can't recognize.

Lake I

We play our flutes as we cross to the far shore
And the sun is setting as I see off my friends
Turn and look back over the lake –
White clouds curl on the blue hills.

Willow Waves

The two rows of perfect trees
Fall reflected in the clear ripples
And do not copy those by the palace moat
Where the spring wind sharpens the good-bye.

The Rapids by the Luans'

Howl howl autumn wind rain
Fast fast stream over smooth rocks
Waves leap and crash together
White egrets startled then down again.

Gold Dust Spring

Drink daily at the Gold Dust Spring, even a little
And live a thousand years, and then the car
Of the green phoenix drawn by the striped dragon
With the feather canopy, to the Jade Emperor's court.

White Stone Shallows

In the clear White Stone Shallows
Green reeds almost near enough to touch
The people on both sides of the river
Wash their silk here under the shining moon.

North Hill

North Hill north of the lake
Red balcony bright among the various trees
Twisting winding the river to the south
Gleaming vanishing by the edge of the green woods.

Bamboo Grove House

I sit alone in the dark bamboos
Play my lute and sing and sing
Deep in the woods where no one knows I am
But the bright moon comes and shines on me there.

Magnolia Slope

Lotus flowers on branches' tips
Send vermilion through the hills
– The valley house deserted, no one there –
Everywhere everywhere they are flowering and falling.

Lacquer Garden

No proud official that man of the past –
Incompetent for secular concerns
The small post he achieved only obliged
His wandering among some such trees.

Pepper Garden

A cassia cup to welcome the Child of God
Wild herbs to offer to the lovely girl
Libation of pepper sauce on the jewelled mats
All to draw down the Lord Within the Clouds.

This sequence is perhaps Wang Wei's most famous and characteristic work, and a number of the individual poems recur in many anthologies. Each of the twenty scenes described was depicted by Wang Wei on his Wang River Scroll, of which now only late paraphrases survive. The twenty corresponding poems by P'ei Ti appear in collected editions of Wang Wei but they are notably inferior. An English translation of them may be found in *Poems of Solitude* by Jerome Ch'en and Michael Bullock, pp. 55–75.

Wang Wei's house here had previously belonged to the distinguished poet, Sung Chih-wen, who died in 712, and to whom the first poem may be taken to allude – as well as to Wang Wei himself.

Apricot Wood House. The notion of the clouds forming in the rafters is taken from a fourth-century Poem of the Travelling Immortals, and so this is fancied to belong to the immortals.

Bamboo Hill. Tsuru is surely right in saying that this poem is an allusion to the Four White Ones, four worthies who took refuge from the savagery of the Ch'in régime on Mount Shang, one of the Chungnan range – a woodman would not be sufficiently erudite to have similar thoughts.

Willow Waves. It was customary to break off a piece of willow to give to a departing traveller. Many partings used to take place by the palace moat.

Gold Dust Spring. There was a myth that a daily drink of powdered gold or jade would confer an exceptionally long and entirely healthy life; this spring was no doubt yellow in colour.

The 'green phoenix' car was that of the Mother of the King of the West, one of the immortals, and the Jade Emperor, the supreme deity in the popular Taoist pantheon.

Magnolia Slope. To emphasize the vivid effect of the flowers, Wang Wei has adapted a line from the *Ch'u Tzu* (*Elegies of Ch'u*), where the notion of lotus flowers growing on trees is illustrative of an impossibility.

32

Lacquer Garden. This poem refers to the Taoist mystic, Chuang Tzu, who is supposed to have flourished about 300 B.C. and to have had charge of such a garden.

Pepper Garden. This poem is largely made of small fragments of *The Nine Songs*, a section of the *Elegies of Ch'u*. These were songs of shamans trying to induce the descent of various divine beings. The reason for making this poem in this way must simply be the mention of pepper sauces in the first of the Nine Songs. See Hawkes, p. 36.

ch. 13

Song of the Peach Tree Spring

A fisherman sailed up a river
                    he loved spring in the hills

On both banks peach blossom
                    closed over the farther reaches

He sat and looked at the red trees
                    not knowing how far he was

And he neared the head of the green stream
                    seeing no one

A gap in the hills, a way through
                    twists and turns at first

Then hills gave on to a vastness
                    of level land all round

From far away all seemed
                    trees up to the clouds

He approached, and there were many houses
                    among flowers and bamboos

Foresters meeting would exchange
                    names from Han times

And the people had not altered
                    the Ch'in style of their clothes

They had all lived near
> the head of Wuling River

And now cultivated their rice and gardens
> out of the world

Bright moon and under the pines
> outside their windows peace

Sun up and among the clouds
> fowls and dogs call

Amazed to hear of the world's intruder
> all vied to see him

And take him home and ask him
> about his country and place

At first light in the alleys
> they swept the flowers from their gates

At dusk fishermen and woodmen
> came in on the stream

They had first come here
> for refuge from the world

And then had become immortals
> and never returned.

Who, clasped there in the hills,
> would know of the world of men?

And whoever might gaze from the world
                    would make out only clouds and hills

The fisherman did not suspect
                    that paradise is hard to find

And his earthy spirit lived on
                    and he thought of his own country

So he left that seclusion not reckoning
                    the barriers of mountain and stream

To take leave at home and then return
                    for as long as it might please him.

He was sure of his way there
                    could never go wrong

How should he know that peaks and valleys
                    can so soon change?

When the time came he simply remembered
                    having gone deep into the hills

But how many green streams
                    lead into cloud-high woods –

When spring comes, everywhere
                    there are peach blossom streams

No one can tell which may be
                    the spring of paradise.

This poem was written by Wang at the age of nineteen. It is based on a tale told in prose and verse by the very celebrated poet, T'ao Yüan-ming, for whose work Wang had great admiration and natural sympathy. Though T'ao tells the tale in a matter-of-fact way and says the event occurred in his lifetime, A.D. 372–427, Wang has made something symbolic out of it; he often alludes to it, in this sense, in other poems. The ancestors of these secluded people were alleged to have taken refuge from the troubles of the Ch'in period, 221–207 B.C., which was followed by the establishment of the Han dynasty in 206 B.C. A translation of T'ao Yüan-ming's prose version is given in appendix II, p. 143.

ch. 6 old style

The Monastery of the Stone Gate
in the Lant'ien Hills

The sun was going down, hill and water were lovely
I idled my boat along, trusted a wind for home
I was too happy to notice how far I had come
And so I arrived right at the head of the stream
I was enjoying the far beauty of clouds and trees
When first I wondered if I had missed my way
How could I know that the clear stream would turn
And go into the hill in front of me?
So I left my boat and took a light stick
And wandered off happy in what I came on
A group of four or five old priests
Far away in the shelter of oaks and pines
Morning lessons there before the woods were lit
Nightly contemplations when the hills were again quiet
The spirit of their rule reached the shepherd boys
For news of this world they would ask a passing woodman
In the darkness under the great trees
They lit incense, lay down on holy mats
And fragrances of valleys scented clothes
And the moon in hills shone on sheer rocks

Not to risk losing the way there on a second search
I should be up at daybreak to climb that way again
Good-bye, friends of Peach Tree Spring
When the flowers are red I shall be there once more.

For the Peach Tree Spring, see preceding poem.

ch. 3   old style

38

Sent away to Chichou

Junior officials easily get into trouble
And here am I packed off to Chichou
The authorities keep strictly to the rules
An enlightened sovereign will not wish things so –
Villages stand along the rich valley
Sea fog is thick over the land –
If ever I do get back from here
How I shall repine at this time's ravaging my hair.

Chichou: a town in Shantung.

   On graduation at the age of twenty-three, Wang was appointed Assistant Secretary for Music (Ta-Yüeh-Ch'eng), for which his great musical talents fitted him, but soon, for some minor dereliction of duty, he was demoted to a small post in Shantung.

ch. 9

Marching song

The bugle is blown and rouses the marchers
With a great hubbub the marchers rise
The wailing notes set the horses neighing
As they struggle across the Golden River
The sun dropping down on the desert's rim
Martial sounds among smoke and dust
We will get the rope round that great king's neck
Then home to do homage to our Emperor.

ch. 2   old style

Three songs for the Lady Pan

Fireflies pass across jewelled windows
Voices have ceased in the golden palace
One stays up through the autumn night, gauze-curtained
And a solitary light gleams on.

*

Autumn's weeds thrive in the palace yard
His Majesty pays no gracious visit now
How unbearable the imperial music
When the golden carriage drives on past that gate.

*

Strange, the ladies' apartments are all shut –
They have left the court, no one to be met with
They have all gone to their spring garden
Sounds of laughter and talk among the flowers.

The Lady Pan was a favourite of the Han emperor Ch'eng-ti (37–2 B.C.) but her humble birth and the slander of a rival caused her to fall from favour. She became a lady-in-waiting to the empress. Her case became a frequent theme for poets. The last of these quatrains is much anthologized, in spite of surprising disagreement among commentators as to its meaning.

ch. 13

Written on a spring evening in
a bamboo pavilion for Sub-prefect Ch'ien,
returning to Lant'ien

Night still, day's movements cease
Dogs can be heard barking beyond the wood
Yes, I remember the other habitations
Were far west of my valley in those hills
You are lucky to be off at sunrise
To that mushroom-picking sinecure.

Sub-prefect Ch'ien was the distinguished poet Ch'ien Ch'i.

Lant'ien was a prefecture south-east of Ch'angan, the capital, in the Chungnan foothills, where a number of Ch'angan gentry had country places.

ch. 2   old style

With the hunt

Bow strings singing in the strong wind
The general hunts near Wei city
Grass dead – the falcons' sight is sharper
Snow gone – the horses' tread light
Quickly we are past Hsinfeng
And back at Hsiliu camp
Behind, where we have shot our game, I see
A thousand miles all calm evening clouds.

ch. 8

Suffering from the heat

Red sun filled sky and earth
Clouds of fire massed into mountains
Vegetation all burnt and shrivelled up
Rivers and lakes all quite dry

Lightest silk felt too heavy to wear
Densest trees gave only wretched shade
Straw mats were unapproachable
Linen was washed three times a day

My thoughts went out of the world
To somewhere utterly alone
Far winds came from a thousand miles
Rivers and seas washed impurities away
Now I realized, the body is the affliction
At last I knew, my mind has never awakened
Here is the way to Nirvana, the gate
To pass through to the joy of purity.

Line 13. 'The body is the affliction': the poet has understood the truth
of the *Tao Te Ching*, ch. 13: 'The reason that we have great affliction is
that we have bodies. Had we not bodies, what affliction would we have?'
  In the following lines the language is Buddhist, not Taoist.

ch. 4   old style

Lament for Meng Hao-jan

I can never see my old friend again –
The river Han still streams to the east
I might question some old man of his place –
River and hills – empty is Tsaichou.

Meng Hao-jan was a distinguished poet, some ten years Wang's senior,
who died in 740. Wang is said to have written this lament on his way
to South China on an official mission. The two poets' work had much
in common, and their names are often associated.

Tsaichou: Meng's native place, an island in the river Han.

ch. 13

Three poems

I live by the river at Meng harbour
My door faces the mouth of Meng harbour
Ships from the south are always arriving –
Is there a letter for me?

*

You've just come from my village
You must have news of my village –
That winter plum outside her curtained window –
Tell me, had it flowered when you left?

*

I see the winter plum is out
And I hear the birds singing again
I am sick at heart to see the spring weeds
And dread they may grow to my door.

The first and third of these poems should be read as the complaints of women whose husbands are away on business. The second represents the thoughts of such a husband.

I think that the winter plum, an early-flowering variety, must have some symbolic significance, but I have not been able to identify this.

ch. 13

A good-bye

Our parting in these hills is over
The sun sets and I shut my door
The spring will be green again next year –
Will my good friend come back too?

The second couplet, like the last couplet of the poem on p. 75 q.v., is based on the *Chao Yin Shih* or *Summons for a gentleman who became a recluse* in the *Ch'u Tzu*, with particular reference to the following lines in Hawkes's translation (op. cit., p. 119):

> A prince went wandering
> And did not return
> In spring the grass grows
> Lush and green.

ch. 13

Reply to Chang Yin

I have a cottage in the Chungnan foothills
The Chungnan mountains face it
All the year long no guests
        and the gate remains shut

All the day long no plans
        and I remain at leisure

Nothing to stop you taking a drink
        or casting for a fish

You have only to come along
        come and see me here.

Chang Yin: a poet of repute.

ch. 6   old style

The Green Stream

To get to the Yellow Flower River
I always follow the green water stream
Among the hills there must be a thousand twists
The distance there cannot be fifty miles
There is the murmur of water among rocks
And the quietness of colours deep in pines
Lightly lightly drifting water-chestnuts
Clearly clearly mirrored reeds and rushes
I have always been a lover of tranquillity
And when I see this clear stream so calm
I want to stay on some great rock
And fish for ever on and on.

ch. 3   old style

Lines

Light cloud, on the pavilion a small rain
Remote cloister, at noon still shut
Sit and regard the colour of the green moss
That seems it will merge up into one's clothes.

ch. 1§

Written at my house near the Wang River at a time of incessant rain

Incessant rain, silent woods,
                smoke rising slow

From fires cooking dinner
                for the men on the land to the east

Vast vast the water fields
                where the white egrets fly

Dark dark the summer trees
                where the yellow orioles sing

In the hills I study peace
                watch the morning mallows fade

Fast under the pines
                pick the dew's new sunflowers

These old countrymen and I
                are equals now —

And need even the seagulls
                still mistrust me?

In line 7 there is allusion to a story from the Taoist classic, *Lieh Tzu*. A certain Yang Tzu-chü was rebuked by Lao Tzu for giving himself airs. He took the rebuke so much to heart that by the time he came to leave the inn where he had been staying, the deference with which he had been greeted on arrival had quite ceased, and people were actually pushing him off his own mat. (The last part of this line means literally: 'struggle mat cease'.)

Line 8 is also an allusion to a *Lieh Tzu* story. A certain man who lived by the sea was fond of seagulls and would go down to the beach every morning to amuse himself with them. One day his father said he wanted to catch one, and went down to the beach with that intention the following day. But the gulls flew high in the sky and would not come near him.

Lines 3 and 4 are the subject of some critical controversy. Though literary allusion, involving mild plagiarism, is an essential feature of Chinese literature, some critics feel that here Wang Wei, always particularly inclined to plagiarize, has gone too far. He has taken two successive five-syllable lines from the T'ang poet, Li Chia-yu, and tacked on a pair of reduplicated expressions at the beginning (vast vast, dark dark). But it is also argued that he has greatly enhanced the feeling of two otherwise banal descriptive lines.

ch. 10

The distant evening view when the weather has cleared

The sky has cleared and there is the vast plain
And so far as the eye can see no dust in the air
There is the outer gate facing the ford
And the village trees going down to the mouth of the stream
The white water shining beyond the fields
The blue peaks jutting behind the hills
This is no time for leisure on the land –
All hands at work in the fields to the south.

ch. 4   old style

Good-bye to Tsu the Third
at Chichou

Smiles of meeting turned to parting tears,
Sad house, and town impenetrably dead
Far mountains sharp on the cold sky
Long river racing in the dusk
Boat cast off and you sailed away
Beyond my gaze, while I still stand.

Tsu the Third is a polite name for Wang Wei's particular friend, Tsu
Ying – third of his family.
   The original poem has eight lines, the first four of which are here
much compressed into the first two.

ch. 4   old style

FOUR POEMS ABOUT CLOUD VALLEY, THE ESTATE OF HUANG-FU YUEH

Birds calling in the valley

Men at rest, cassia flowers falling
Night still, spring hills empty
The moon rises, rouses birds in the hills
And sometimes they cry in the spring valley.

Lotus Flower Bank

Off every day to pick the lotuses
Far to the island, often back in the dusk
Plying the pole but careful not to splash
Afraid to wet the lotus's red array.

Cormorant Dam

There down among the red lotuses
Up again soaring over the clear bank
Then how sleek as it perches alone there
Fish in beak, upright on a drifting log.

Duckweed Pool

In spring the pool is deep and wide
You must be waiting for the light boat to come back
When the shifting green duckweed will close behind
And the willow branches sweep it apart again.

ch. 13

Good-bye to Adjutant P'ing T'an-jan

You don't yet know the road to the frontier
Once more P'an Ch'ao's footsteps will be followed –
Where the yellow clouds cut off spring's colours
And the horns call up the frontier's sadness
The Gobi is more than one year's separation
And the river forks out over the boundary
You will soon be teaching those foreign envoys
How to drink from King Yüeh-chih's skull.

P'an Ch'ao: a famous general of the Later Han dynasty, whose victories over the Hsiung-nu (? = Huns) earned him the title of Marquis of Ting-yüan (= Distant Pacification).

   Yüeh-chih: a Hsiung-nu king of Han times, whose skull was made into a drinking cup by the victorious Chinese.

ch. 8

Written at Command in reply to the Emperor's spring-detaining poem on the distant spring view in the rain, on the way from the Magic Palace to the Pavilion of Joy

The river Wei of itself encircled
                Ch'in's frontiers with its bends

The Yellow Mountains of old surrounded
                Han's palace with their slopes

The imperial carriage passes far out
                from the willows at the Immortals' Gate

From the high portico He looks back
                at the flowers in His park

In the clouds the Imperial City and
                the Pavilion of the Twin Phoenixes

In the rain the spring trees and
                the habitations of His subjects –

He uses the positive elements
                to rule as the time requires

He does not make this Progress
                because He values the beauty of things.

'Spring-detaining poem': a poem in which the beauties of spring are dwelt on and the passing of spring, like that of a parting guest, regretted.
  Ch'in dynasty: 221–207 B.C.

Han dynasty: 206 B.C.–A.D. 220.

Yellow Mountains: Huang-shan; among the many mountains thus named, these are those of Shensi, where there was a Yellow Mountain Palace in Han times.

This poem is a pre-eminent specimen of the court poetry required by the Emperor on many occasions from his entourage. It is a technical *tour de force,* a series of parallel couplets, rigidly obedient to the rules of tonal counterpoint, densely packed with meaning. But there is no feeling behind such feats of sycophantic virtuosity.

ch. 10

For Tsu the Third

A spider hangs in the empty window
Crickets sing on the front steps
The cold wind of the year's evening is here –
How are things with you now, my friend?

Your high house is empty, uninhabited
There are no words for this separation
Your front gate is out of use, shut
And the declining sun shines on autumn weeds

Even if I soon had news of you
Miles of river and pass stay interposed –
I did once visit Ju and Ying
And last year I went back to my old hills

Can twenty years of friendship
Not achieve one day more?
You are deep in poverty and illness
And hardships begin to close over me

Even if you are not back by mid-autumn
Make sure of autumn's end at the latest
How many days to that glad meeting
Is what I think of all day long.

ch. 2   old style

Good-bye

Dismount and we'll take a drink together
Where are you off to?
You say you've failed – retiring
To the foot of the Southern Mountains?
Well, go – and no more questions
For the white clouds there'll never be an end.

This poem, one of Wang Wei's most famous, is generally regarded by commentators as a kind of soliloquy, but there can be no certainty on this point.

ch. 3   old style

Lament for Yin Yao

We followed you back for your burial
                    on Mount Shihlo

And then through the greens of oaks and pines
                    we rode away home

Your bones are there under the white clouds
                    until the end of time

And there is only the stream that flows
                    down to the world of men.

                                        ch. 14

For Ch'iu Wei at parting

You are saddled up to go beyond the white clouds
To wind and twist among the mountains ahead
Today and the next day
I know I shall not be calm
I send off your excellency with this poem
Longing for the orioles among the flowers again
And I glance back with each slow step
Slow to approach this gate so near.

ch. 3   old style

Return to the Wang River

Distant bell sounding at the mouth of the valley
Fewer and fewer the fishermen and woodmen
Away in the far mountains it is evening
And I am going alone towards the white clouds home
Water-chestnut flowers so delicate so hardly still
Willow catkins so light so easily fly
Colours of spring on the banks of the marsh to the east
And I am melancholy as I shut my door.

ch. 7

In return for Mr Yang's poem on spending the evening on the Lute Terrace, and ascending to the library in the morning

Brush dust from ancient texts and read
Take a lute, wait for the moon, and play
By the Peach Stream where the Han are unknown
Under the pines which retain their ranks from Ch'in

In the empty valley few come home
The blue hills are turned from the sun, cold
I envy you your refuge in this place
Long view to the white clouds' rim.

For the Peach Stream see p. 34.

Some pine trees were said to have been ennobled by the first Ch'in emperor (221–209 B.C.) for giving him shelter when caught in a storm during a ceremonial ascent of Mount T'ai.

ch. 7

A greeting from the mountains to my younger brothers and sisters

There are in these hills many monks
Who group in recital and meditation
Gaze from your city walls into this distance
All that you will see is the white clouds.

'Brothers and sisters' may simply mean fellow Buddhists of both sexes, rather than members of the poet's family.

ch. 13

In answer to Forestry Officer Su, who called at my Lant'ien retreat and met no welcome

My humble house at the mouth of the valley
Tall trees round a remote village
A stony track diverted your carriage
To my door in the hills – and who answered it?
Fishing boats fast to the frosty bank
Hunters' fires glowing on the wintry plain
And from beyond the white clouds only
The distant bell and the monkeys' nocturne.

ch. 7

Poem of the Melon Garden

From the pavilion high up in my melon garden there is a lovely view down to the Southern Mountains. Two or three of my friends and I wrote poems on the subject and had other excellent versifiers do the same. The rhyme word was 'garden' and there was no requirement as to length. It was Hsieh Ch'ü, tutor to the Crown Prince, who led off with this title, and the rest of us followed with our poems on it.

Just off to hoe my melons one day
– The hoe was in my hand – I heard knocking at the gate
Elegant postilions leading carriage horses
The proper escorts of smart equipages
Shouts and calls along the narrow lane –
And suddenly my old friends were with me.
I led them where a cool breeze would blow
To relax and look upon the heaven and earth.

Rich rich the Emperor's demesnes
And all the palaces, how resplendent
The imperial road emerging from the wood
The palace roofs all brandishing bright flags.

But our prime longing lay in the blue hills
And to keep the company of the white clouds
In the turning wind, rain there west of the city
In the cross-light, villages there on the plain.

At first we filled our cups with wine
And then on and on listened to pleasant talk
While yellow orioles sang in the deep trees
And red hibiscus glowed in the middle of the garden.

And I shall still want my friends under the pines
When I sit on a rock and listen to the pleasant monkeys.

ch. 2   old style

The Chungnan Mountains

T'ai-i nearly touching the Citadel of Heaven
Chain of hills down to the edge of the sea
White clouds closing over the distance
Blue haze – nothing comes into view
The central peak transforms the whole tract
Dark and light the valleys, each way distinct –
If I want a lodging for the night here
Across the river there's a woodman I may ask.

T'ai-i and the Citadel of Heaven are stars as well as a mountain and the imperial capital respectively. The whole tract refers not only to an area of land but also to the stars above it, which control it climatically and so on.

ch. 7

Going up to the Temple of Perception

Path through bamboos up from the First Stage
Towards the Magic City out above lotus peaks
Through a window, there is all of Ch'u
Over the trees the Kiukiang plain
Cross-legged, soft grass beneath
Tones of Sanskrit sounding among tall pines
Up in the Void beyond the Cloud of the Law
Contemplating, achieving Nirvana.

The visit to the temple is described with the terminology of the development of a bodhisattva into a Buddha, in the Ten Stages. The Cloud of the Law is the Tenth Stage. The Magic City is an illusory state of Nirvana. The cross-legged position is that of contemplation.

ch. 8

Living by the river Ch'i

I am living in seclusion by the waters of the Ch'i
The land to the east is bare and without a hill
The sun is hidden beyond the mulberry trees
The river shines between the villages
Shepherd boys move off towards their far hamlets
Hunting dogs follow their masters home
And what has the man without occupation done?
He has passed the whole day behind his closed gate.

ch. 7

Going at dawn to the Pa Pass

Just at dawn I set off for Pa Pass
With the last of spring I remembered the capital
In the bright river a woman was washing
With the morning sun all the birds sang
Water country, markets on boats
Mountain bridges up among the tree tops
I climbed and hundreds of villages emerged
And in the distance two rivers shone
The people spoke a peculiar dialect
But the orioles sounded as in my own country
And luckily I know about landscape
And that abated my feeling of isolation.

ch. 12

Inscription for a friend's mica screen

This screen of yours unfolded
Against that wild courtyard
Can show you hills and springs
Uncontrived with paint.

This poem is said to be Wang Wei's earliest known, written when he was fifteen. It is exceptionally light and simple in texture.

ch. 13

On leaving the Wang River retreat

At last I put my carriage in motion
Go sadly out from the ivied pines
Can I bear to leave these blue hills ?
And the green stream – what of that ?

ch. 13

In the hills at nightfall in autumn

In the empty hills just after rain
The evening air is autumn now
Bright moon shining between pines
Clear stream flowing over stones
Bamboos clatter – the washerwoman goes home
Lotuses shift – the fisherman's boat floats down
Of course spring scents must fail
But you, my friend, you must stay.

See note p. 47.

ch. 7

End of spring near the river Ssŭ

It was near Kuangwu City
                  I met the end of spring

A traveller returning from Wenyang
                  handkerchief wet with tears

Silent silent falling flowers
                  birds crying in the hills

Green green the willows
                  at our crossing place.

ch. 14

Facing the high watchtower
A farewell to Commissioner Li

We part and I see from the tower
The river plain all dusk
The sun down and the birds flying home
The traveller on away.

The title is from the collection of songs known as *yüeh-fu*, which date from the early Han dynasty, and were frequently imitated by T'ang poets.

ch. 13

Waiting for Hsü Kuang-i who did not come

Double gates open early in the morning
I was up and listening for the sound of a carriage
Hoping to hear the tinkle of your belt
When I would go straight out to welcome you
The evening bell has rung in the emperor's garden
Sparse rain is crossing the spring city
I realize that we shall not see each other –
Back in my house still hoping – but in vain.

ch. 9

Giving P'ei Ti a drink

I will pour you some wine
               and you must relax

Human feelings turn over and over
               like the waves of the sea

Friends who have gone grey together
               may still reach for their swords

And the first with vermilion doors
               may mock those cap in hand

Colours of grasses all arise
               from the wet of a little rain

Buds are on the point of opening –
               and the spring wind is cold

The world's affairs and the floating clouds –
               why question them?

You had best take life easily –
               and have a good dinner.

One may suppose that P'ei Ti is visiting his friend in a state of great anger and dissatisfaction at his failure to obtain high office. Line 3 may conceivably imply that the two friends have been quarrelling about this.
    Line 4. 'Vermilion doors': the colour of the doors of high officials.
    Line 5. Insignificant people succeed.
    Line 6. People with promise of distinction (i.e. P'ei Ti) sometimes fail through no fault of their own.

ch. 10

Presented to the Duke of Shih-hsing

Rather perch in a wild wood
Rather drink from a mountain stream
Than consume fine rice and meat
And struggle for audience of the great

How crude this vulgar frugality
But I shall dress coarsely till my head is white
Intelligence may not be my forte
But I may claim to be humane

They say that Your Excellency
Makes no distinction of friend and foe
That you do not sell offices
That all your activities are for all the people

Your humble servant thus petitions you:
Could he find a place in your ministry
With gratitude for choice on public ground
Without desire for private preference.

Duke of Shih-hsing: Chang Chiu-ling, prime minister at this time
(734), a poet of note, and a friend of Wang Wei, who now received an
appointment.

ch. 5   old style

To the Prefect Wei Chih

Desolation of an abandoned city
Void of a thousand miles of river and hill
Far up in the sky an autumn sun
Cries of wild geese that return
Withered grass gleaming on the wintry bank
Last paulownia littering the courtyard
With this the evening of the year is come
And I look at it all and hum 'The Sad Old Man' –
My friend is not to be seen there
East of the desolate forest vast on the plain.

'The Sad Old Man': a song from the Han period.

ch. 2   old style

A walk on a winter day

I walk out of the city by the eastern gate
And try to send my gaze a thousand miles
Blue hills crossed with green woods
Red sun round on the level plain
North of the Wei you get to Hantan
East of the Pass you go out to Han valley
This was where the Ch'in demesnes met
This was where the governors came to court
The cocks called in Hsienyang
And officers of state struggled for precedence
Ministers called on noblemen
Dukes assembled for official banquets
But Hsiang-ju became old and ill
And had to retire alone to Wuling.

Hsienyang: the capital under the Ch'in dynasty, 221–207 B.C.

  Hsiang-ju: Ssu-ma Hsiang-ju, 179–117 B.C., a famous writer to whom Wang Wei is venturing to compare himself.

ch. 4   old style

Passing the mountain cloister of the holy man, T'an-hsing, at Kanhua Temple

In the evening he took his fine cane
And paused with his guests at the head of Tiger Stream
Urged us to listen for the sound in the mountains
Then went along by the water back to his house
  Profusion of lovely flowers in the wilds
  Vague sound of birds in the valley
When he sits down tonight the empty hills will be still
And the pine wind will suggest autumn.

Tiger Stream: a certain hermit about the end of the fourth century is related to have lived in a temple, near which was a stream. If ever he escorted visitors back beyond this stream, the roar of a tiger would be heard, so that he normally avoided going beyond it. But on one occasion, deep in conversation with T'ao Yüan-ming (see note on p. 37) and another friend, he inadvertently went too far. The roar of the tiger was duly heard and the three men burst out laughing, and then parted. The hermit then built the Pavilion of the Three Laughs.

ch. 7

Living in the hills

In calm loneliness I shut my door
Against the whole afterglowing sky
Cranes are nesting in all the pines
No visitors at my wicket gate
Tender bamboos with the new bloom on them
Red lotuses shed of their old garments
A lamp shines out at the ford
Water-chestnut pickers come home.

ch. 7

Drifting on the lake

The autumn sky is clear into the distance
The clearer so far from human habitation
On a sandy shore a crane, or beyond clouds
A mountain top makes my content
The limpid ripples calm and evening comes
The moon shines out and I relax
Tonight my single oar takes over
As I drift without thought of going back.

ch. 9

In the hills

White rocks jutting from Ching stream
The weather's cold, red leaves few
No rain at all on the paths in the hills
Clothes are wet with the blue air.

This poem is not certainly by Wang Wei, in that it does not appear in his original collected works. But it is wholly characteristic of him, and we have the weighty opinion of the great Sung poet, Su Tung-p'o (Su Shih), for this attribution. Su Tung-p'o, discussing a painting by Wang Wei called 'Mist-rain at Lant'ien', on which a slightly different version of this poem was inscribed, said, 'When I savour Wang Wei's poem, the picture is in the poem. When I look at the picture, the poem is in the picture. This poem is by Wang Wei.' The words 'the picture is in the poem' have come to be used in the sense of 'there is a picture in the poem' in respect of any successfully graphic quatrain.

ch. 15

Seeing off Chang the Fifth back to the hills

I see you off and I am all grief –
Who is it after all I am seeing off?
How many days have we been arm in arm?
And now one morning you shake out travelling clothes
I have a small house in the eastern hills
Would you mind cleaning up its wretched entrance?
Because I too shall resign soon and be off –
One cannot force oneself against one's heart.

ch. 4   old style

Return to Mount Sung

The river ran clear between luxuriant banks
And my carriage jogged along on its way
And the water seemed to flow with a purpose
And in the evening the birds went back together –
Desolate town confronting an old ford
Setting sun filling the autumn hills
After a long journey, at the foot of Mount Sung
I have come home and shut my door.

ch. 7

Seeing off Ch'en Tzu-fu to the east of the Yangtze

Under the willows at the ford
                there are few travellers left

As the boatman steers away
                to the other curving shore

But my thoughts will follow you
                like the spring's returning colours

Returning from south of the Yangtze
                back to the north.

ch. 14

On a portrait of Ts'ui Hsing-tsung

I painted you once when you were young
Now you have become an old man
A new acquaintance now
Will know that in the old days you were fine.

ch. 13

Staying a night at Ch'engchou

I left the metropolitans in the morning
And here I am with the people of Ch'eng for the night
When he has no friends in some place
The solitary traveller makes one of his servant
I have peered in vain for Nanyang and Loyang
Over the plain dark with long autumn rain
The old farmers are home by the edge of the fields
While the boys are guarding the herds in the wet
The landlord lives on the rise to the east
His house surrounded with the season's crop
Insects humming, looms at rest
Birds twittering, grain coming ripe
Tomorrow I must cross Ching River
Last night I was still in Golden Valley
I am going away – what do I mean by it?
I am off to the end of the earth for a little pay.

ch. 4   old style

To Prime Minister Chang at Chingchou

Where are my thoughts after all?
Far off in Chingchou – there my sad gaze turns
In all the world I have had no other friend
Whose kindness to remember all my life
I mean soon to belong to the country, and sow
And plant things, and grow old in my refuge
I watch the wild geese southwards out of sight
And think how I may send a word to you.

This was presumably written in 737, when Chang Chiu-ling was demoted and sent to a provincial post, ostensibly for having sponsored a person who eventually incurred the death penalty.

There was a myth that wild geese – and fish – could carry messages.

ch. 7

Written in my country garden in spring

On my roof spring pigeons call
And round the village almond trees bloom white
Men take axes to cut the high branches
Shoulder hoes to inspect the conduits
Returning swallows know their old nests
The old resident scans the new calendar
About to drink I suddenly hold my hand
With a pang for a friend on a far journey.

ch. 3   old style

Visiting Hsiangchi Temple

I didn't know Hsiangchi Temple
And went miles into cloudy peaks
Between ancient trees, no tracks of man –
Where was that bell deep in the hills ?
Sound of a stream choking on sharp rocks
Sun cool coloured among green pines –
At dusk beside a deserted pool, a monk
Meditating to subdue the poisonous dragon.

'The poisonous dragon' represents the evil passions.

ch. 7

94

On a mission to the frontier

Off in a single carriage on my mission to the frontier
For dependencies beyond Chüyen now
I am carried like thistledown out from the Han defences
And wild geese are flying back to the savage waste
From the Gobi one trail of smoke straight up
In the long river the falling sun is round
At Hsiao Pass I meet our patrols
Headquarters are on Mount Yenjan.

Wang Wei went on this mission in 737.
 Chüyen: Hsiung-nu territory conquered by the Han.
 Mount Yenjan: scene of a famous victory in the first century A.D.,
thus implying that the patrols brought good news.

ch. 9

Song of the Kansu frontier

Two miles galloping all the way
Another one plying the whip –
A message arrives from headquarters
The Huns have surrounded Chouch'üan
The frontier passes are all flying snow
Beacons are out, no smoke.

ch. 2   old style

In answer to Assistant Magistrate Chang

In my late years I only like
Tranquillity, the world's affairs
No longer exercise my mind
Which I now find unpolicied.
Back into the old woods where
Pine winds flutter my loose sash
Hill moon lights me at my lute –
This is all my knowledge. If
You ask me for a principle
Of poverty and riches, listen
The Fisherman's Song comes clear to the shore.

The Fisherman's Song is found both in the *Mencius* and in the *Ch'u Tzu* or *Elegies of Ch'u*. The allusion here is presumably to the latter context. Ch'ü Yüan, a poet of the fourth century B.C., to whom the poem is traditionally though wrongly attributed, explains to a fisherman why he is wandering in exile by the river: the world is dirty, he alone is clean; everyone is drunk, he alone is sober, and so on. The fisherman finally rows away, singing, 'How clean the river water – I will wash my feet.' That is to say, one's behaviour should be adapted to whatever conditions prevail (see Hawkes, op. cit., pp. 90–91).

ch. 7

Detaining Ts'ui Hsing-tsung
to say good-bye

Hold your horse for our good-byes
How clear and cold by the palace moat
How lovely those hills ahead of you
What a grief you are going off alone.

ch. 13

Looking out on the snow in late winter, and remembering the hermit Hu

Cold when the drum sounds for dawn
Bright the mirror where I inspect my haggard face
Beyond the shutter bamboos clatter in the wind
Open the door and there's the snow filling the hills
Down from all the sky bringing the deep lanes peace
White drifts making the courtyards still
I wonder what is happening in Yüan An's house –
Are you calmly there behind closed doors?

In the last two lines Wang Wei compares his friend Hu with a certain Yüan An of antiquity, who stayed in his house during a time of heavy snow and consequent famine, in order not to complicate the task of those who brought relief; the official rescuers saw that he had cleared no path from his house, and found him inside, rigid with cold and hunger.

ch. 7

Farmer

The last crop will soon be done
Prospects for the next not known
The old man now takes to rice gruel
And at the year's end has almost no clothes
Birds feed their young by the mossy well
Fowls call from the white board cottage roof
He hitches his lean mare to a decrepit cart
Or, straw shod, feeds his bristly pig
The pomegranates break with the heavy rain
The taro leaves swell with early autumn
He takes his food out to the fields, rests under the mulberries
Or comes back to the grass beside his house
The place where he lives is called Fools' Valley
Who cares whether well so named?

ch. 11

For Ts'ui the Ninth, leaving for the Southern Mountains: recited to him on horseback, at parting

Shake hands by the city wall
When will we meet again?
There are cassia flowers in those hills
Don't wait for their snow fall.

ch. 13

The Lady of Hsi

Present love could not efface
Memory of what once she enjoyed
She looked at a flower with eyes tear-filled
And spoke no word to the king of Ch'u.

It was related that in 680 B.C. the ruler of the state of Ch'u overthrew that of Hsi and seized its queen, who, out of loyalty to her former husband, and in spite of bearing children to her second, never spoke to the latter.

This poem was written at the order of Prince Ning, half-brother of the emperor Hsüan-tsung, in the following circumstances: Prince Ning, though possessed of some ten or so wives, fell in love with the wife of a near-by pastry-cook, to whom he gave liberal gifts in exchange for his wife. A year later, in the presence of a number of distinguished literary guests, of whom Wang Wei, at twenty, was probably the youngest, the prince asked the pastry-cook's wife whether she still loved her former husband, but she made no answer. The pastry-cook was sent for, and when his wife saw him, her eyes filled with tears. The company, much affected by the scene, was asked to compose poems on it. Wang Wei's was the first to be finished, and it was so good that it was agreed that the others should give up.

A flower is a recognized symbol for a lover.

ch. 13

Light lines on a flat rock

Dear flat rock
> facing the stream

Where the willows are sweeping
> over my wine cup again

If you say that the spring wind
> has no understanding

Why should it come blowing me
> these falling flowers?

ch. 14

Good-bye to Yüan the Second on his going on a mission to Anhsi

In Wei city the morning rain
                    has settled the light dust

At the inn it is green green
                    with the new willow leaves

I beg you to drink down
                    another cup of wine

You're going out west of the frontier
                    and you've no friends there.

This poem achieved great fame and popularity beyond the circle of those who read poetry, when set to music as a song of farewell. One of the items in Ezra Pound's *Cathay* is based on this poem.

ch. 14

Remembering my brothers east of the mountains on the ninth of the ninth month

Here I am alone
                    in a strange place a stranger

And always this festival
                    revives thoughts of my people

From far I know my brothers
                    are climbing some high place

All crowned with dogwood
                    their number one short.

Written at the age of seventeen, when Wang Wei was studying in Ch'angan.

ch. 14

Good-bye to Li, Prefect of Tzŭchou

In endless valleys trees reaching to the sky
In numberless hills the call of cuckoos
And in those hills half is all rain
Streaming off branches to multiply the springs —
The native women will bring in local cloth
The men will bring you actions about potato fields
Your revered predecessor reformed their ways
And will you be so bold as to repudiate him?

Tzŭchou, in Szechwan, a region inhabited by non-Chinese people.
　The predecessor was Wen Weng, an enlightened governor of the region in Han times, who checked the barbarity of local customs and civilized them in the Chinese manner.

ch. 8

Lamenting white hairs

Once a child's face
                now an old man's

White hairs soon replace
                the infant's down

How much can hurt the heart
                in one life's span

We must turn to the gate to Nirvana
                where else can we end our pain?

ch. 14

Farewell to Inspector Wei

You are off after the general
               to capture the enemy king

Deserts of sand, horses galloping
               towards Chüyen

Far off you will know our messengers
               out beyond Hsiao Pass

And anxiously sight the lone fort
               over near the setting sun.

Chüyen: see note on p. 95. As in that poem, allusion is made to campaigns of the Han period. The 'enemy king' is named in the original Yuhsien, a Hsiung-nu king, who in 132 B.C. allowed himself to be surrounded by Han troops, because he was too drunk to notice it. He broke out of the ring but many of his chieftains were captured.

ch. 14

For P'ei Ti, while we were living quietly by the Wang River

Cool hills more deeply green
Sound of autumn streams all day
We lean on our sticks outside my rustic door
And listen windward to cicadas of evening
Sun still sinking over the ford
Up from the village a single fire's smoke
And here's another Chieh-yü drunk
Madly singing in front of Five Willows.

Chieh-yü: a man of the state of Ch'u, in the time of Confucius, who
feigned madness and lived as a recluse to avoid public service, and urged
Confucius to do the same. The word 'madly' in the last line alludes to his
designation as the 'madman of Ch'u' in the *Analects*.

Five Willows: the name given to his house in the country by T'ao
Yüan-ming (for whom, see note on p. 37); he was much given to drink-
ing bouts.

ch. 7

On the line, 'The autumn sun lets fall a pale radiance'

The great void, the cool sky is calm
Crystal brilliance, the white sun is autumn
The round light contains all things
And its broken image enters the quiet stream
Far up and uniting with the blue depths
Away and down floating with the river plain
The shades at noon make all the trees distinct
The slanting light falls on the high houses
Sung Yü climbed up and resented it
Chang Heng looked into the distance and grieved
But if that last glow can be trusted
Will those paths in the clouds be sad, sad?

The line in the title is from a poem by Chiang Yen (444–505) called 'Distant View of the Ching Mountains'. The immediate context is:

> 'On the cold frontier no shadow to be seen
> The autumn sun lets fall a pale radiance
> A mournful wind dishevels the thick forests
> The clouds are red, the river rising cold.'

'Sung Yü' was the supposed author of the *Chiu Pien* or *Nine Arguments*, which appear in the *Ch'u Tzu* or *Elegies of Ch'u*. This cycle of poems opens, in Hawkes's translation (op. cit., p. 92):

> 'Alas for the breath of autumn!
> Wan and drear, flower and leaf fluttering fall and turn to decay
> Sad and lorn! as when on journey far one climbs a hill and looks down on the water to speed a returning friend
> Empty and vast! the skies are high and the air is cold!'

Chang Heng (78–139) is better known as a writer of *fu* or rhyme-prose, but he also wrote lyrics. The commentators say that the allusion here is to his *Poems of the Four Griefs*. It is true that these poems are elaborately melancholy but they contain no direct reference to autumn. The third line of each of the four poems is of the form:

'I turn and gaze far eastwards and my tears wet my pen'

Only the direction and the article wetted alter in the subsequent poems. It is to these lines that the commentators see allusion. A French translation of the four poems appears in *Anthologie de la poésie chinoise classique*, pp. 86–7.

ch. 15

Living quietly by the Wang River

Now that I am back in my retreat
I no longer go to the Green Gate
I often lean against a tree in front of my house
And look away to the villages down on the plain
Where the green oats are reflected in the water
And the white birds circle towards the hills —
And I think of the Man of Yüling
Watering that garden from the well.

The Green Gate: one of the gates of Ch'ang-an.

  The Man of Yüling was the style adopted by a certain Chung-tzu
of the state of Ch'i, during the period of the Warring States (481–221
B.C.). He disapproved of the corrupt administration of his brother and
went into retirement at Yüling. In spite of lavish offers from the king of
Ch'i, who wanted him to return and be prime minister, he took on the
job of watering someone's garden.

ch. 7

Visiting the forest pavilion of the recluse, Ts'ui Hsing-tsung, with Lü Hsiang

The green trees give layers of shade
in all directions

The green moss thickens daily
and so there is no dust

He sits legs outstretched hair unkempt
under the tall pines

And regards with the whites of his eyes
the rest of the world.

Ts'ui Hsing-tsung was a cousin of Wang Wei's.

Lü Hsiang was a distinguished poet, with whom Wang Wei often exchanged compositions.

The last line alludes to the poet Juan Chi (A.D. 210–63), one of a group of scholars and poets known as The Seven Sages of the Bamboo Grove, who lived a secluded life, and is said to have regarded the many people he despised in the manner described.

ch. 14

Good-bye

I see you off to the southern shore
                my tears like threads

Off you go to the eastern provinces
                and cause me grief

You can tell them there
                that their old friend is haggard

No longer what he was
                in those Loyang days.

The first line is a notable instance of plagiarism. The first four characters come straight from a *fu* or piece of rhyme-prose by Chiang Yen (for whom see first note on p. 110), while the final three come from a poem by the emperor Wu of the Liang dynasty (464–549).

ch. 14

While interned in Bodhi Temple, the poet was visited by P'ei Ti, to whom he recounted how the rebels would make music on Deep-Green Lake, with a company of artists, and how he himself would weep at it. He secretly composed this dirge, and recited it to P'ei Ti.

Citizens become like mists in the wilds
                  and the heart breaks

When will the officers of state ever
                  come again to court?

From autumn sophora trees leaves fall
                  in desolate palaces

While on Deep-Green Lake they
                  make their music.

This poem is said to have helped to save the poet's life when, after the rebellion of 755–7, he was charged with collaboration. The poem has no title but appears with the preface, as above, in the collected works.

ch. 14

Another oral composition for P'ei Ti

How can we escape from these earthly toils
Shake off the dust and leave the noise of the world
And gently swinging a thorn stick
Get home to the Peach Blossom Stream?

Said to have been composed on the same occasion as the preceding poem, hence the title.

For the Peach Blossom Stream see pp. 32–7.

ch. 13

To repay my friends for their visit

Ah, I have not died
I have grief in my life here alone
Retired to Lant'ien
With a little plot to till myself
Taxes paid at the year's end
And offerings for my ancestors
Dawn walks to the eastern hill
In a dew still wet on the grass
Evening sights of fires' smoke
And laden people coming home

I hear that I have guests
And I have my poor entrance swept
What can I give them to eat?
Slice a melon, pick some jujubes

Beside my honoured guests
I am prematurely grey
I am ashamed at my lack of good mats
And have to provide coarse ones

We can climb that floating bank
And pick those lotuses
Or tranquilly look at the silver sturgeon
Or watch the shadows on the white sand

Birds in the hills all flying
Sun dimmed by a light haze
You mount your carriages and horses
And suddenly scatter like rain

Fledgelings twitter in the deserted village
Fowls cry by the empty house
I am back in my deep solitude
Renewed sadness, redoubled sighs.

This poem may have been written soon after the death of Wang Wei's wife, which occurred when he was thirty. He never remarried.

The poem is in lines of four syllables, probably the most ancient Chinese metre, but not common at this date.

ch. 1   old style

Four poems on the pleasures of the country

Picking water-chestnuts, at the ferry head the wind is sharp
Walking with a stick, west of the village the sun slants
That fisherman is at the Place of the Apricots
Those houses are in the valley of the Peach Blossom Stream.

*

Dense, dense fragrant herbs, autumn's green
Down down tall pines, summer's cool
Sheep and cattle return on their own along the lanes
Young children do not recognize the signs of office.

*

Below the hill one trail of smoke, distant village
At the sky's rim a single tree on the high heath land
There's a one-gourd Yen Hui in that mean lane
There's a Master of Five Willows in that house opposite.

*

Peach flowers again full of the night's rain
Willow green once more clad in spring's haze
Flowers have fallen, the house boy has not yet swept
Orioles are singing, the visitor in the hills sleeps on.

Place of the Apricots: it is related that Confucius used to teach and make
music at the Place of the Apricots, perhaps an island in a lake. One day a
fisherman, attracted by the music, came ashore and listened attentively.
Confucius then respectfully begged this wise hermit for instruction.

Peach Blossom Stream: see p. 34.

One-gourd Yen Hui: Yen Hui was one of Confucius' favourite
disciples. The reference here is to the following passage of the *Analects*
(Book VI, section 9):

'The Master said: Incomparable indeed was Hui! A handful of rice to eat, a gourdful of water to drink, living in a mean street – others would have found it unendurably depressing, but to Hui's cheerfulness it made no difference at all.'

The above is quoted from Waley, *The Analects of Confucius*, p. 117.

Master of Five Willows: the poet T'ao Yüan-ming (see p. 37).

These four poems are six-syllable *chüeh-chü*. The metre is unusual, giving a distinctive heavy and jerky effect, there being caesurae between the first pair of syllables and the second, and between the second and the third. I hope that this will be apparent to the reader in at least some of the lines of these versions.

ch. 14

Sitting alone on an autumn night

I sit alone sad at my whitening hair
Waiting for ten o'clock in my empty house
In the rain the hill fruits fall
Under my lamp grasshoppers sound
White hairs will never be transformed
That elixir is beyond creation
To eliminate decrepitude
Study the absolute.

ch. 9

Calling on Li I

Colours of autumn weeds at the front gate
No carriages all day long
When I, a stranger, enter the lane
Dogs bark under the cold trees
His unbrushed hair is sometimes not pinned up
And he still carries books on the Way as he walks about
He has ideas like mine, this man
Who rejoices in the Way, is content to be poor
A drink of Ich'eng wine, and then
I go back to my own place of retreat.

'The Way': the commentators take this to mean Taoism, but in view of Wang Wei's known and definite Buddhist beliefs, it is surely more likely to mean Buddhism. The character, *tao* = the Way, more usually means Taoism, but unfortunately it frequently means Buddhism instead.

ch. 3   old style

Watching a farewell

Green green the willowed road
The road where they are separating
A loved son off for far provinces
Old parents left at home

He must go or they could not live
But his going revives their grief
A charge to his brothers – gently
A word to the neighbours – softly
A last drink at the gates
And then he takes leave of his friends

Tears dried, he must catch up his companions
Swallowing grief, he sets his carriage in motion
At last the carriage passes out of sight
But still at times there's the dust thrown up from the road

I too, long ago, said good-bye to my family
And when I see this, my handkerchief is wet with tears.

ch. 4 old style

Lament for Yin Yao

What is a man's life span?
In the end he returns to formlessness
I think how you too have died
And how much there is to afflict a man's heart
Your good mother still unburied
Your one daughter only ten years old
In the cold vastness beyond the walls
I hear desolate the sound of lamentation
Floating clouds make the expanse of the skies
Birds fly and do not sing
That traveller – how lonely
And even the sun gleams cold.

I remember how when you were still alive
You asked me to teach you about the absolute
And I encouraged you but now I grieve
That I was dilatory and so you failed –
All your friends have made you offerings
And these also are too late for your lifetime
Not along one way only did I fail you –
And I am weeping as I go back home.

ch. 5   old style

Peasants by the River Wei

Slanting light making the village shine
Herds and flocks returning along the lanes
Old peasants thinking of the shepherd boys
Leaning on sticks and waiting at cottage doors
Pheasants calling where the wheat is growing strong
Silkworms sleeping now few mulberry leaves are left
Labourers shouldering hoes come in
And exchange a glance and an easy word –
Here is the peace and seclusion I long for
And I intone the Soldiers' Lament.

What I have called the 'Soldiers' Lament' is to be found in the *Shih Ching*, the most ancient compilation of Chinese verse:

> 'How few of us are left, how few!
>   Why do we not go back?
>   Were it not for the prince and his concerns
>   What should we be doing here in the dew?
>
>   How few of us are left, how few!
>   Why do we not go back?
>   Were it not for the prince's own concerns
>   What should we be doing here in the mud?'

Translated by Waley, *The Book of Songs*, p. 113.

ch. 3   old style

Middle-aged, much drawn to the Way
Settled for my evening in the Chungnan foothills
Elation comes and off I go by myself
Where are the sights that I must know alone
I walk right on to the head of a stream
I sit and watch when clouds come up
Or I may meet an old woodman –
Talk, laughter, never a time to go home.

ch. 3   old style

Crossing the Yellow River on the way to Ch'ingho

Sailing in a boat in the great river
Waters mounting to the edge of the sky
Sky and waves suddenly part
And there was a city vast and populous
And on we went and there were more towns
And mulberry trees and flax between them
I looked back towards my old place –
A waste of waters right up to vaporous clouds.

ch. 4   old style

On going up to Ch'inglung Temple and looking towards the Lant'ien Hills, after parting with my brother Chin

Another parting on the road
Dark the vastness all around
I mounted high and did not see you
And my hills too were beyond clouds
Distant trees screened the traveller
The autumn pass vanished in the far sky
I am sad and wonder where your duties
Are sending you flying to now.

ch. 4   old style

Taking the cool of the evening

Thousands of trunks of huge trees
Along the thread of a clear stream
Ahead the great estuary over which
Comes the far wind unobstructed
Rippling water wets white sands
Silver sturgeon swim in transparency
I lie down on a wet rock and let
Waves wash over my slight body
I rinse my mouth and wash my feet
Opposite there's an old man fishing.
How many fish come to the bait –
East of the lotus leaves – useless to think about it.

East of the lotus leaves: presumably a reference to an old song where occur the lines:

> 'Fish play east of the lotus leaves,
> Fish play west of the lotus leaves.'

So that the last couplet probably refers to those who needlessly get caught up in the world's affairs, out of greed.

ch. 4   old style

In the garden in spring

Nightlong rain, I put on my clogs
Spring cold, I wear my old overcoat
White water spreads through the open dykes
Red peach flowers show between the willow trees
The grassy borders make a chess board
At the wood's edge rise the poles of the wells
I go back indoors and take up my desk
And evening will come, and I'll be alone among my weeds.

ch. 7

On being visited in late spring
by Mr Yen and his friends

Pines, chrysanthemums along my wild paths
Books, cartloads of them in my house
Sunflower seeds cooked to regale the honoured guests
Come to my poor house on their bamboo viewing
Birds sitting before the spring is green
Orioles singing on after the flowers have fallen –
I am sad at this final whitening of my hair
And doubly grudge the season's glory.

ch. 7

For P'ei Ti

We've not seen
We've not seen each other now
For a long time.
Each day at the head of the stream
I remember us there arm in arm
Arm in arm, at one we were –
And memory renews
The pain of the sudden good-bye.
If today's memory is thus
How deep was feeling then.

The first couplet of the original consists of a three-syllable line and a five-syllable line; thereafter the lines are all of five syllables, though they are rendered irregularly here.

ch. 2 old style

For P'ei Ti the Tenth

Lovely the landscape in the setting sun
You and I writing poems together
Calmly gazing into the far emptiness
Chins resting on our as-you-like-its
Spring wind shifting all the grasses
Scented orchids growing in my hedge
Dim dim the sun warms my room
A farmer comes along to have a talk
Joy joy spring has returned to the marshes
Calm calm the water has formed pools
Though the peaches and plums are not yet in flower
There are buds all over the branches
Please get your stick, ready to go back –
May I tell you that the busy season is upon us.

'As-you-like-it': this is intended to render *ju-i*, which is a common
expression meaning 'at will' or 'as desired'. Here it designates a Bud-
dhist emblem, originally a short sword, which developed into an object
about twenty inches long, one end of which was fashioned in the form of
a stylized hand, for use as a backscratcher: that is to say, one can scratch
any part of one's body, otherwise inaccessible, as one likes. These objects
could be very ornate, made out of a variety of rich materials.

ch. 2   old style

For Censor Ch'ao returning home to Japan

Massed the waters, limitless
How to know what is east of the Immortals' Ocean
In all the world what place is so far?
Ten thousand miles like riding the void
Heading to your country, you can only look to the sun
Your returning sail can merely trust to the wind
The Great Turtle's body turning the sky black
The fishes' eyes piercing the waves with red
Your country's trees are beyond Fusang country
My friend, you will be in your lonely islands
Separated, we will be in different realms
How are tidings to pass between us?

Censor Ch'ao: this is Ch'ao Heng, the Chinese name of the Japanese Abe no Nakamaro (698–770). This man was sent to China as a student in 716, lived there all his life, and died there in 770. The present poem was written in 753, when Nakamaro had been given leave to return home; however, as happened too frequently, his ship was wrecked off South China, whence he eventually returned to the capital. He had a number of friends at court and among poets, notably Li Po. Two Chinese poems attributed to him appear in a large anthology, but some, needlessly, I think, doubt their authenticity.

During the seventh and eighth centuries Japan acted vis-à-vis China much as she has done during the last century or so vis-à-vis Europe and America, strenuously attempting, with a good deal of success, to adopt and adapt all the elements of an alien civilization. Large numbers of students were dispatched from time to time, generally to return if they escaped shipwreck, after a more or less long sojourn, laden with learning and books and religious articles.

Immortals' Ocean: the islands of the Immortals were supposed to lie a long way to the east, supported by the Great Turtle (line 7).

'In all the world': this renders *chiu-chou* or, in Japanese, *kyū-shū*, meaning the nine provinces or regions into which China, and so the world, was supposed to have been divided in ancient times. At least one

134

Japanese commentator thinks this refers to Kyūshū, the large southernmost island of Japan, but I can find no evidence that this appellation was yet in use, the island being still known as Tsukushi.

Fusang: a country supposed to exist far to the east, named after the gigantic twin-trunked trees called *fusang* supposed to grow there. The word came to be used eventually, by both Chinese and Japanese, as a name for Japan (read Fusō in Japanese).

This poem is preceded by an unusually long, elaborate, panegyrical preface, of nearly six hundred characters. It would be unintelligible without several pages of annotation, and I have therefore omitted it.

ch. 12

Song for a friend going home to the mountains

The man of the mountains	wants to go home
Clouds dark dark	rain driving down
Waters surging	green rushes swaying
White egrets suddenly	wheeling about
My friend you must not	hitch up your clothes
Mountains many layered	all one cloud
Heaven and earth confused	indistinguishable
Trees dim and dark	air heavy
Monkeys not seen	only heard
Suddenly west of the mountains	evening light
We see among the eastern fields	a distant village
Flat plain green	a hundred miles clear
I am sad	thinking of you

This song is in the song-style of the *Ch'u Tzu* or *Elegies of Ch'u*. The gap in the lines above is filled in the original by a meaningless syllable, now pronounced *hsi*, intended, according to Hawkes (op. cit., p. 5), 'to carry the singing voice through parts of the melody for which there were no corresponding words'.

ch. 1   old style

Sitting alone on an autumn night, thinking of my cousin, Ts'ui Hsing-tsung

Night still day's movements cease
Cicadas singing, on and on
In my courtyard's sophoras, a north wind sounds
Day and night, it is high autumn now
I think of you preening your feathers
Ready to float up to the clouds
My time of life will soon be white hair
And in the year's evening I think of the fairy shores
As you hurry about from dawn to dusk
You wouldn't care to join me at South Field.

'South Field': a phrase from the *Shih Ching* or *Book of Songs*, which came to be used simply for the country, as opposed to the town.

ch. 2 old style

Light lines on my Wang River retreat

Willow branches sweeping the ground –
                              not worth cutting

Pine trees touching the clouds
                              and growing further still

Wistaria soon giving darkness
                              for monkeys to hide in

Oak leaves so abundant
                              I might keep musk-deer.

'Not worth cutting': for fencing the neglected vegetable garden.
    Musk-deer eat oak leaves.
    Kobayashi (op. cit., p. 231) suggests that this poem describes the
neglected condition of his estate on his return in 742 from five or six
years of provincial duties, during which his mother had lived there alone.

ch. 14

Thoughts on a winter night

The winter dark is cold and also long
The night clock strikes within the palace
Grass is white, clouded over with frost
Trees are decayed, lit up by the clear moon
Rich raiment bright beneath a gaunt face
Vermilion candles shining on white hairs
The Han emperor rather honoured youth
When I look in the mirror, I'm ashamed to go to court.

'The Han emperor': it is related that the emperor Wu (140–86 B.C.) once visited his secretaries' office, and there noticed a very old man. He asked the old man when he had become a secretary, to which the reply was: 'Your servant became a secretary in the time of the emperor Wen (179–156); the emperor Wen liked literary matters, your servant, military. Then came the emperor Ching (156–140) who liked handsomeness, while your servant is ugly. When your majesty came to the throne, you liked youth, but I was already old. So it is that I have failed in three successive reigns and grown old in the secretariat.' The emperor was much moved and promoted the old man.

ch. 5   old style

Lines

With age I am growing too lazy to write verses
And now old age is my only company
In a past life I was mistakenly a poet
In a former existence I must have been a painter
Unable to throw off my remnant habits
I find the world has come to know me for them
My name and style – these they have right
But this heart of mine they still do not know.

The first four lines of this poem appear in a certain collection of T'ang quatrains (*chüeh-chü*) and are there said to have been used to head the Wang River Scroll (for which, see pp. 27–33).

ch. 5　old style

APPENDIX I

A letter to P'ei Ti from the hills

THIS twelfth month the weather has been bright and agreeable, and I could have come over the mountain, but I hesitated to disturb you, deep as you are in the Classics. So I went off for a walk in the hills. I rested at the Kanp'ei Temple, where I had something to eat with the hill monks, before I left and went north over the Black Water. The clear moon lit up all the country. In the night I went up Huatzu Hill, and the waters of the Wang River were rippling up and down with the moon. Distant lights in the cold hills were coming and going beyond the woods. The barking of the winter dogs in the deep lanes sounded like leopards. The pounding of grain in the village could be heard between the strokes of a distant bell. Now I am sitting by myself. The servants are asleep. I am thinking a lot about old days, our composing poems as we walked arm in arm along steep paths beside clear streams.

We must wait for the spring, when all the grasses and trees will come out again and we can look at the spring hills. The light dace coming out of the water. The gulls soaring. Dew wetting the green banks. The morning call of the pheasants in the corn. All this is not far off, and then you can surely come and wander about with me? If it weren't for your natural genius, I would of course not impose anything so inessential on you. But it holds deep interest. No urgency. This goes t o you by a hillman. No more now.

From Wang Wei, man of the hills.

APPENDIX II

The story of the Peach Blossom Spring by T'ao Ch'ien (T'ao Yüan-ming)

DURING the T'aiyüan period of the Ch'in dynasty there was a man of Wuling who lived by fishing. He went along a stream and forgot how far he had gone. Suddenly he found himself in a forest of peach blossom extending several hundred paces along both banks, unmixed with any other sort of tree. The fragrance was lovely, and fallen petals were everywhere. The fisherman was extremely surprised, and continued onwards in the hope of reaching the limit of this forest. The forest ended at the source of the stream. There he came on a hill, and in the hill a small opening, from which there seemed to come some light. So he abandoned his boat and went through the opening. The passage was at first so narrow that a man could only just pass, but after going some fifty paces or so, he found that it widened out into a broad and bright place. On the level ground there were dignified buildings, as well as good ricefields, fine pools, mulberry trees and bamboos. There were roads and lanes criss-crossing, and the sounds of fowls and dogs could be heard. People were coming and going, busy sowing seed, and the clothes of both the men and the women looked foreign. Both the grey-haired elders and the youngest children had an air of natural happiness.

They were much amazed at the sight of the fisherman, and asked him where he had come from, to which he replied fully. They then took him back to one of their houses, put wine before him, killed a fowl, and gave him a meal. When news of this man became known in the village, they all came along to find out about him. They said of themselves that their ancestors, escaping from the troubles of the Ch'in period, had brought away their wives and children and the other inhabitants of their locality to this isolated place, and that subsequently no one had left there. This had led to their being cut off from those outside. They asked what dynasty there was now, they themselves having no knowledge of the Han dynasty, not to mention those of Wei and Ch'in. The fisherman replied fully and precisely to their questions, and they were all dumbfounded. The others all came and invited the man to their houses, and all gave him food and drink. He stayed for several days before taking his leave and departing. The people had meanwhile told him that there was no object in divulging their existence to others.

When he emerged, he regained his boat and retraced his route, noting it at every turn. When he reached the prefecture, he went to the prefect and told his tale. The prefect thereupon dispatched someone to go with him and find the route he had noted, but they lost their way and could not find it again.

Liu Tzŭ-chi of Nanyang, a man of quality, heard the tale and was eager to go off to the place himself. But before anything had been achieved, he was taken ill and died, and since then no one has looked for the stream.